The Sayings of Oscar Wilde

The Sayings of

OSCAR
WILDE

edited by

HENRY RUSSELL

with an introduction by

JOHN BAYLEY

DUCKWORTH

Seventh impression 1994
First published in 1989 by
Gerald Duckworth & Co. Ltd.
The Old Piano Factory
48 Hoxton Square
London N1 6PB

Introduction and editorial arrangement
© 1989 Gerald Duckworth & Co. Ltd

ISBN 0 7156 2305 2

British Library Cataloguing in Publication Data

Wilde, Oscar *1854–1900*
  The sayings of Oscar Wilde
  I. Title. ·   II. Russell, Henry
  828'.802

  ISBN 0-7156-2305-2

Designed by Peter Guy

Photoset in North Wales by
Derek Doyle & Associates, Mold, Clwyd
Printed in Great Britain by
Redwood Books, Trowbridge, Wiltshire

Contents

Introduction

by John Bayley

Warton Professor of
English Literature at Oxford

LIKE JOY, humour has to be caught on the wing. Oscar Wilde, who had read everything though he wore his scholarship so lightly, might have amused himself by recoining Blake's famous aphorism. He who kisses the joke as it flies lives in eternity's sunrise. There is never anything ponderous about the Wildean wisdom. And Oscar would have enjoyed coupling the erotic with the ephemeral, and setting both in the immortal pantheon of art.

'To love oneself is the beginning of a lifelong romance.' What could be at once more true and more false, more dangerous and more lighthearted, than that? But it is thrown out in the third act of *An Ideal Husband* without, as it were, a care in the world. Wilde would never have written a work of fiction (*The Picture of Dorian Gray* is a bundle of mischief and perception, not a novel) because he would have had to show the implications of such a remark working themselves out. He was far too intelligent not to have done so. But he preferred to leave his audience to do the work of drawing their own conclusions for themselves. It was his way not so much of flattering his hearers as of paying them the compliment that they saw things as he did, as immediately but also as comprehensively.

Wilde's wit is never pretentious. In the context of the theatre or the drawing-room it is quite happy to raise its laugh and to pass on to the next jest. He would never, like his near contemporary Nietzsche, have assembled his sayings to illustrate a philosophy and a *Weltanschauung*. 'Thus Spake Oscar' would merely have been one more joke. But when his *mots*, his thoughts, his more calculated sayings, are collected as intelligently as Henry Russell has done it in this book, they reveal a mind and a man as fascinating as could be found anywhere in the annals of thinking and living. It takes a complete Wilde like this to show us both how good the epigrams are, and how good they are at concealing and making light of the graphic history they none the less reveal.

For Wilde in his best art was not a serious person. Richard Ellmann's incomparable Life pays him the compliment he would have been the first to smile wryly at, and to set aside: that of taking him too seriously as a great, humane, ultimately almost a saintly figure. He was none of those things, as they are usually understood in relation to the good and the great, and he would not appeal as he does if he had been. To invoke Nietzsche again, his appeal lies in being 'human, all too human'. And something more than that. Loving oneself is an all too human characteristic, and often leads to loving others, to their happiness and to one's own. A perfect romance in fact. Wilde's tragedy was that he did not love himself enough; that he loved, like Othello, not wisely but too well. The lifelong romance turned into a tragedy that was also a brutal farce. He was not kind enough to himself, which is the road to at least one sort of wisdom, and the famous saying in *The Ballad of Reading Gaol* – 'For each man kills the thing he loves' – is an ironic untruth in relation to its author. If Wilde had loved himself more he would not have destroyed himself.

That destructive element gives a resonant background to what can only be described as the kindly lightheartedness of most of these jests. The contrast gives them their strange authority. Their truth comes from the fact that human beings have to live in two worlds: one willed and active and competitive; the other more obscure, passive and involuntary. In the first we show off in some degree, exercise all the frivolity of display. In the second we are the victims of forces that lie below the surface, too determined and too complex to understand. Wilde's epigrams are in one sense an assertion of gaiety over fatedness, of the humour of keeping lively over the destiny of giving into things.

Most humour recognises this contrast, and Wilde's more than most. A striking feature of Henry Russell's admirably comprehensive selection is how it brings out Wilde's friendliness to, and understanding of, women, always the principal actors and sufferers in the drama of display and victimisation, desire and necessity. It is usually insufferable when men – and men who are authors – talk 'understandingly' of women, but I don't think any woman would object to the remarks Wilde makes about them, or find them in the least patronising. They are saved by their fellow-feeling – the man could only make them by knowing what it is to be in the same boat – as much as by their lack of solemnity. Wilde was not always kind: hardly anybody is, as he himself might have said, and his behaviour to his wife Constance was, towards the end, not nice at all. He seems to have stopped thinking about her or being aware of her, a with-drawal of the premises of love, or even affection, so total that it must have helped to destroy her as much as him.

But to hold that against him would be to play the part of being censorious, and censoriousness is the unwitting enemy of all he wrote. Unwitting because Wilde never seems deliberately to set out to mock it, or to proclaim himself as its opponent. Like Jane Austen's character when confronted by the observations of a stupid man, Wilde does not bestow on the censor in all of us the compliment of rational opposition. He simply, and rightly, makes another joke. But complete awareness lurks beneath the joke. 'Every

woman is a rebel, and usually in revolt against herself.' He knew what he was talking about, and never
more so than when he allows the joke to carry itself
away, as it were, into the gracefulness of apparent
absurdity. 'All women become like their mothers.
That is their tragedy. No man does. That is his.' The
notion of a man failing to become like his mother is
wonderfully comic, yes, and it seems as if the epi-
grammatist was merely concerned to make his wit
swallow its tail. But no, the implications go on and
on. Men ought to be more like women, to have their
qualities; but those qualities are themselves over-
conditioned by the demands of a woman's life. Hardy
was making the same point at about the same time,
and much more laboriously, in his last novel, *The
Well-Beloved*, in which an emancipated young woman
is shown beginning to repress her own daughters just
as her mother did. But Hardy did not add the joke
about the man, which turns the superior observer
into the comic-shameful role of participant.

'There is only one real tragedy in a woman's life.
The fact that her past is her lover, and her future
invariably her husband.' Again the wit naturally
transposes itself, and applies – though with a complete absence of heavy tragic irony – to all human life.
But don't let's pretend. 'There is always something
infinitely mean about other people's tragedies', as
Lord Henry Wotton remarks in *The Picture of Dorian
Gray*. As social animals we know our friends are not
like Macbeth or Othello, but we have a sneaking
desire to be a bit like those tragic heroes ourselves.
Other people's tragedies being mean goes with scandals about them being more interesting. 'I love scandals about other people,' says Lord Henry, 'but
scandals about myself don't interest me. They have
not got the charm of novelty.' Lord Henry, like his
creator, is not self-centred enough to be a villain.

Max Beerbohm was very fond of Wilde but was
unable to take him seriously as saint or martyr, and

that inability tells us a lot about the real nature of Wilde's talents, and those of Beerbohm too. Neither writer could do what Sir Walter Scott called 'the big bow-wow stuff': both might have said, with Jane Austen, 'Let other pens than mine dwell upon guilt and misery.' When Wilde was forced into guilt and misery, and felt himself impelled to dwell among them, and upon them, his writing becomes for the first time subtly insincere. Sincerity is mainly a matter of talent, as Aldous Huxley remarked in the style of Wilde himself, and Wilde had no talent for a direct confrontation with the abyss. His literary genius preferred to go bunburying. His wit and wisdom could get in the whole of life, but on their own terms. Lord Henry remarked that he could stand brute force, 'but brute reason is quite unbearable. It is hitting below the intellect.' Wilde's epigrams never do that.

Beerbohm must have appreciated what must be called the unexpectedly domestic side of his friend's wit. 'I love simple pleasures. They are the last refuge of the complex.' And a very good one too. Wilde's funniest paradoxes very often refer to the simplest things, the most universal human weaknesses. Every day on the radio or in the papers we hear some commentator doing what a Wildean paradox has defined and pinned down unforgettably. They are washing their clean linen in public. They know that their apparently artless admissions of loss of memory, domestic incompetence, lateness at the office, inability to play golf, and so on and so forth, will help to endear them to the listener or the reader. They know, as we all do, that there is nothing much wrong about ourselves really, that we are good, decent sort of people; but it is one of the commonest traits in human nature to seem to enjoy owning up to our faults; and it took the wit of Wilde – his own good-nature too – to perceive the process and exactly define it. The context is of course *The Importance of Being Earnest*, and the 'scandalous' fact that so many women in London enjoy seeming to flirt with their own husbands. They are washing their clean linen in public.

It is worth noticing that Wilde perceives and comments on human nature much less portentously than the French professionals of the seventeenth and eighteenth centuries, Vauvenargues, La Bruyère and La Rouchefoucauld. Their apophthegms have a ponderosity about them; they are all too obviously intended to be admired, and admire themselves, throughout the history of great literature. Even G.K. Chesterton, who paid Wilde the sincere compliment of imitation, is in his brilliance much more emphatic and pretentious than his master. Wilde would never have laid down, like La Rochefoucauld, that 'in the misfortunes of our best friends there is something that does not altogether displease us'; just as he would never have sunk to Chesterton's coy little *mot* about those who do not have the Faith and therefore cannot have the Fun. No; to repeat what I suggested earlier, it is our own novelists, and especially our domestic novelists – Jane Austen, Somerville and Ross, Elizabeth Bowen – who are most in tune with Wilde's wit and wisdom. He was himself a great friend of Ada Leverson, whom he called 'the Sphinx', and who may herself have coined the phrase 'a sphinx without a secret'. I strongly recommend her novel *The Little Ottleys*, one of the funniest and most discerning novels of its own or any period. Wilde may have suggested some of the things in it, just as she may have been the source of some of the jokes and situations in his own work. Neither of them were in the least possessive or proprietary about the products of their own perception and intelligence; and that lack of exclusiveness is itself one of the best things about Wilde's humour. Like Falstaff he is not only funny himself but the inspiration of fun in others.

Women

No woman should ever be quite accurate about her age. It looks so calculating.

The Importance of Being Earnest
ACT FOUR

One should never trust a woman who tells one her real age. A woman who would tell one that, would tell one anything.

A Woman of No Importance
ACT ONE

With a proper background women can do anything.

Lady Windermere's Fan
ACT TWO

'What do you call a bad man?'
'The sort of man who admires innocence.'
'And a bad woman?'
'Oh! the sort of woman a man never gets tired of.'

A Woman of No Importance
ACT ONE

The only way to behave to a woman is to make love to her, if she is pretty, and to someone else, if she is plain.

The Importance of Being Earnest
ACT ONE

Women who have common sense are so curiously plain.

An Ideal Husband
ACT THREE

Man, poor, awkward, reliable, necessary man belongs to a sex that has been rational for millions and millions of years. He can't help himself. It is in his race. The History of Woman is very different. We women have always been picturesque protests against the mere existence of common sense. We saw its dangers from the first.

A Woman of No Importance
ACT TWO

Women are never disarmed by compliments. Men always are. That is the difference between the two sexes.

An Ideal Husband
ACT THREE

There is nothing in the world so unbecoming to a woman as a Nonconformist conscience.

Lady Windermere's Fan
ACT THREE

I am afraid that women appreciate cruelty, downright cruelty, more than anything else. They have wonderfully primitive instincts. We have emancipated them, but they remain slaves looking for their masters all the same. They love being dominated.

The Picture of Dorian Gray
CHAPTER EIGHT

Women never know when the curtain has fallen. They always want a sixth act, and as soon as the interest of the play is entirely over, they propose to continue it.

The Picture of Dorian Gray
CHAPTER EIGHT

Crying is the refuge of plain women, but the ruin of pretty ones.

Lady Windermere's Fan
ACT ONE

A mother who doesn't part with a daughter every season has no real affection.

Lady Windermere's Fan
ACT ONE

All women have to fight with death to keep their children. Death, being childless, wants our children from us.

A Woman of No Importance
ACT FOUR

There's nothing in the world like the devotion of a married woman. It's a thing no married man knows anything about.

Lady Windermere's Fan
ACT THREE

Women have become so highly educated... that nothing should surprise us nowadays, except happy marriages.

A Woman of No Importance
ACT TWO

More women grow old nowadays through the faithfulness of their admirers than through anything else!

An Ideal Husband
ACT ONE

Women love us for our faults. If we have enough of them, they will forgive us everything, even our intellects.

The Picture of Dorian Gray
CHAPTER FIFTEEN

Most women in London, nowadays, seem to furnish their rooms with nothing but orchids, foreigners, and French novels.

A Woman of No Importance
ACT FOUR

Good women have such limited views of life, their horizon is so small, their interests are so petty.

A Woman of No Importance
ACT THREE

It takes a thoroughly good woman to do a thoroughly stupid thing.

Lady Windermere's Fan
ACT TWO

How hard good women are! How weak bad men are!

Lady Windermere's Fan
ACT ONE

If a woman wants to hold a man, she has merely to appeal to the worst in him.

Lady Windermere's Fan
ACT THREE

Women have a wonderful instinct about things. They can discover everything except the obvious.

An Ideal Husband
ACT TWO

Women are not meant to judge us, but to forgive us when we need forgiveness. Pardon, not punishment, is their mission.

An Ideal Husband
ACT FOUR

If you want to know what a woman really means – which, by the way, is always a dangerous thing to do – look at her, don't listen to her.

A Woman of No Importance
ACT THREE

No woman should have a memory. Memory in a woman is the beginning of dowdiness. One can always tell from a woman's bonnet whether she has got a memory or not.

A Woman of No Importance
ACT THREE

All women become like their mothers. That is their tragedy. No man does. That is his.

The Importance of Being Earnest
ACT ONE

Many a woman has a past, but I am told that she has at least a dozen, and that they all fit.

Lady Windermere's Fan
ACT ONE

Every woman is a rebel, and usually in revolt against herself.

A Woman of No Importance
ACT THREE

She certainly has a wonderful faculty of remembering people's names, and forgetting their faces.

A Woman of No Importance
ACT ONE

If a woman really repents, she has to go to a bad dressmaker, otherwise no one believes in her.

Lady Windermere's Fan
ACT FOUR

Men always want to be a woman's first love. We women have a more subtle instinct about things. What we like is to be a man's last romance.

A Woman of No Importance
ACT TWO

Nothing spoils romance so much as a sense of humour in the woman.

A Woman of No Importance
ACT ONE

Twenty years of romance make a woman look like a ruin, but twenty years of marriage make her something like a public building.

A Woman of No Importance
ACT ONE

In the case of very fascinating women, sex is a challenge, not a defence.

An Ideal Husband
ACT THREE

Sphinxes without secrets.

A Woman of No Importance
ACT ONE

Ah! the strength of women comes from the fact that psychology cannot explain us. Men can be analysed, women...merely adored.

An Ideal Husband
ACT ONE

Oh, there is only one real tragedy in a woman's life. The fact that her past is always her lover, and her future invariably her husband.

An Ideal Husband
ACT THREE

Women treat us as Humanity treats its gods. They worship us, and are always bothering us to do something for them.

The Picture of Dorian Gray
CHAPTER SIX

Women represent the triumph of matter over mind; men represent the triumph of mind over morals.

The Picture of Dorian Gray
CHAPTER FOUR

London is full of women who trust their husbands. One can always recognise them. They look so thoroughly unhappy.

Lady Windermere's Fan
ACT TWO

Never trust a woman who wears mauve, whatever her age may be, or a woman over thirty-five who is fond of pink ribbons. It always means that they have a history.

The Picture of Dorian Gray
CHAPTER EIGHT

One should never give a woman anything she can't wear in the evening.

An Ideal Husband
ACT THREE

Wicked women bother one. Good women bore one. That is the only difference between them.

Lady Windermere's Fan
ACT THREE

That is the worst of women. They always want one to be good. And if we are good, when they meet us, they don't love us at all. They like to find us quite irretrievably bad, and to leave us quite unattractively good.

Lady Windermere's Fan
ACT THREE

Young women of the present day seem to make it the sole object of their lives to be always playing with fire.

A Woman of No Importance
ACT ONE

These American girls carry off all the good matches. Why can't they stay in their own country? They are always telling us it is the Paradise of women... That is why, like Eve, they are so extremely anxious to get out of it.

A Woman of No Importance
ACT ONE

American girls are as clever at concealing their
parents as English women are at concealing their
past.

The Picture of Dorian Gray
CHAPTER THREE

I like men who have a future, and women who have a
past.

The Picture of Dorian Gray
CHAPTER FIFTEEN

Men

Is it fair to go back twenty years in any man's career?

A Woman of No Importance
ACT THREE

When men give up saying what is charming, they give up thinking what is charming.

Lady Windermere's Fan
ACT TWO

Men are such cowards. They outrage every law of the world, and are afraid of the world's tongue.

Lady Windermere's Fan
ACT THREE

The husbands of very beautiful women belong to the criminal classes.

The Picture of Dorian Gray
CHAPTER FIFTEEN

The fact is that men should never try to dictate to women. They never know how to do it, and when they do it, they always say something particularly foolish.

The Importance of Being Earnest
ACT THREE

No gentleman ever takes exercise.

The Importance of Being Earnest
ACT TWO

When a man does exactly what a woman expects him to do she doesn't think much of him. One should always do what a woman doesn't expect, just as one should say what she doesn't understand.

The Importance of Being Earnest
ACT THREE

Men become old, but they never become good.

Lady Windermere's Fan
ACT ONE

A man can be happy with any woman as long as he does not love her.

The Picture of Dorian Gray
CHAPTER FIFTEEN

The happiness of a married man...depends on the people he has not married.

A Woman of No Importance
ACT THREE

The home seems to me to be the proper sphere for the man. And certainly once a man begins to neglect his domestic duties he becomes painfully effeminate, does he not?

The Importance of Being Earnest
ACT THREE

The Ideal Man should talk to us as if we were goddesses, and treat us as if we were children. He should refuse all our serious requests, and gratify every one of our whims. He should encourage us to have caprices, and forbid us to have missions. He should always say much more than he means, and always mean much more than he says.

A Woman of No Importance
ACT TWO

If a man is a gentleman, he knows quite enough, and if he is not a gentleman, whatever he knows is bad for him.

The Picture of Dorian Gray
CHAPTER THREE

Men know life too early.

A Woman of No Importance
ACT FOUR

I have always been of the opinion that a man who desires to get married should know either everything or nothing.

The Importance of Being Earnest
ACT ONE

No gentleman ever has any money.

The Importance of Being Earnest
ACT TWO

Men are so very, very heartless. They know their power and use it.

A Woman of No Importance
ACT TWO

All men are married women's property. That is the only true definition of what married women's property really is.

A Woman of No Importance
ACT TWO

By persistently remaining single a man converts himself into a permanent public temptation.

The Importance of Being Earnest
ACT TWO

No man has real success in this world unless he has got a woman to back him, and women rule society.

A Woman of No Importance
ACT THREE

It is a terrible thing for a man to find out suddenly that all his life he has been speaking nothing but the truth.

The Importance of Being Earnest
ACT FOUR

The world was made for men and not for women.

A Woman of No Importance
ACT ONE

Formerly we used to canonise our heroes. The modern method is to vulgarise them. Cheap editions of great books may be delightful, but cheap editions of great men are absolutely detestable.

The Critic as Artist

Mothers, of course, are all right. They pay a chap's bills and don't bother him. But fathers bother a chap and never pay his bills.

The Importance of Being Earnest
ACT ONE

Examinations are of no value whatsoever. If a man is a gentleman, he knows quite enough, and if he is not a gentleman, whatever he knows is bad for him.

A Woman of No Importance
ACT THREE

Love & Marriage

Most people live *for* love and admiration. But it is *by* love and admiration that we should live. If any love is shown us we should recognise that we are quite unworthy of it.

De Profundis

In married life affection comes when people thoroughly dislike each other.

An Ideal Husband
ACT THREE

It's most dangerous nowadays for a husband to pay any attention to his wife in public. It always makes people think that he beats her when they're alone.

Lady Windermere's Fan
ACT TWO

More marriages are ruined nowadays by the common sense of the husband than by anything else. How can a woman be happy with a man who insists on treating her as if she was a perfectly rational being?

A Woman of No Importance
ACT TWO

In married life, three is company and two is none.

The Importance of Being Earnest
ACT ONE

I have often observed that in married households the champagne is rarely of a first-rate brand.

The Importance of Being Earnest
ACT ONE

The bond of all companionship, whether in marriage or in friendship, is conversation.

De Profundis

When one is in love, one always begins by deceiving oneself; and one always ends by deceiving others. That is what the world calls a romance.

The Picture of Dorian Gray
CHAPTER FOUR

The one charm of marriage is that it makes a life of deception absolutely necessary for both parties.

The Picture of Dorian Gray
CHAPTER ONE

Each time one loves is the only time one has ever loved. Difference of object does not alter singleness of passion. It merely intensifies it.

The Picture of Dorian Gray
CHAPTER SEVENTEEN

There is always something ridiculous about the emotions of people whom one has ceased to love.

The Picture of Dorian Gray
CHAPTER SEVEN

An engagement should come on a young girl as a surprise, pleasant or unpleasant, as the case may be.

The Importance of Being Earnest
ACT ONE

I am not in favour of long engagements. They give people the opportunity of finding out each other's characters before marriage, which I think is never advisable.

The Importance of Being Earnest
ACT FOUR

Those who are faithful know only the trivial side of love; it is the faithless who know love's tragedies.

The Picture of Dorian Gray
CHAPTER ONE

It's a curious thing...about the game of marriage – a game, by the way, that is going out of fashion – the wives hold all the honours, and invariably lose the odd trick.

Lady Windermere's Fan
ACT ONE

Love is fed by the imagination, by which we become wiser than we know, better than we feel, nobler than we are: by which we can see life as a whole: by which, and by which alone, we can understand others in their real as in their ideal relations.

De Profundis

Loveless marriages are horrible. But there is one thing worse than an absolutely loveless marriage. A marriage in which there is love, but on one side only; faith, but on one side only; devotion, but on one side only and in which of the two hearts one is sure to be broken.

An Ideal Husband
ACT FOUR

No married man is ever attractive except to his wife.

The Importance of Being Earnest
ACT TWO

When a woman marries again it is because she detested her first husband. When a man marries again it is because he adored his first wife. Women try their luck; men risk theirs.

The Picture of Dorian Gray
CHAPTER FIFTEEN

One should always be in love. This is the reason one should never marry.

A Woman of No Importance
ACT THREE

It's perfectly scandalous the amount of bachelors
who are going about society. There should be a law
passed to compel them all to marry within twelve
months.

A Woman of No Importance
ACT TWO

Men marry because they are tired; women because
they are curious; both are disappointed.

The Picture of Dorian Gray
CHAPTER FOUR

It is the growth of the moral sense of women that
makes marriage such a hopeless one-sided
institution.

An Ideal Husband
ACT THREE

My husband is a sort of promissory note; I'm tired of
meeting him.

A Woman of No Importance
ACT TWO

I really don't see anything romantic in proposing. It is
very romantic to be in love. But there is nothing
romantic about a definite proposal. Why, one may be
accepted. One usually is, I believe. Then the
excitement is all over. The very essence is
uncertainty.

The Importance of Being Earnest
ACT ONE

Romance should never begin with sentiment. It
should begin with science and end with a settlement.

An Ideal Husband
ACT THREE

Who, being loved, is poor? Oh, no one.

A Woman of No Importance
ACT FOUR

The real draw-back to marriage is that it makes one unselfish. And unselfish people are colourless. They lack individuality.

The Picture of Dorian Gray
CHAPTER SIX

The Book of Life begins with a man and a woman in a garden. It ends with Revelations.

A Woman of No Importance
ACT ONE

The amount of women in London who flirt with their own husbands is perfectly scandalous. It looks so bad. It is simply washing one's clean linen in public.

The Importance of Being Earnest
ACT ONE

Girls never marry the men they flirt with. Girls don't think it right.

The Importance of Being Earnest
ACT ONE

Curious thing, plain women are always jealous of their husbands, beautiful women never are. They are always so occupied in being jealous of other people's husbands.

A Woman of No Importance
ACT ONE

Faithfulness is to the emotional life what consistency is to the life of the intellect, simply a confession of failure.

The Picture of Dorian Gray
CHAPTER FOUR

To elope is cowardly. It's running away from danger. And danger has become so rare in modern life.

A Woman of No Importance
ACT ONE

There is nothing, nothing like the beauty of home-life, is there? It is the mainstay of our moral system in England ... without it, we would become like our neighbours.

> *A Woman of No Importance*
> ACT ONE

To love oneself is the beginning of a lifelong romance.

> *An Ideal Husband*
> ACT THREE

Passion makes one think in a circle.

> *The Picture of Dorian Gray*
> CHAPTER SIXTEEN

Youth & Age

To get back my youth I would do anything in the world, except take exercise, get up early, or be respectable.

The Picture of Dorian Gray
CHAPTER NINETEEN

There is nothing like youth. The middle-aged are mortgaged to Life. The old are in life's lumber-room. But youth is the Lord of Life. Youth has a kingdom waiting for it.

A Woman of No Importance
ACT THREE

The youth of the present day are quite monstrous. They have absolutely no respect for dyed hair.

Lady Windermere's Fan
ACT THREE

Youth smiles without any reason. It is one of its chiefest charms.

The Picture of Dorian Gray
CHAPTER FOURTEEN

The old believe everything: the middle-aged suspect everything: the young know everything.

*Phrases and Philosophies
for the Use of the Young*

The only people to whose opinions I listen now with any respect are people much younger than myself.

The Picture of Dorian Gray
CHAPTER NINETEEN

A burnt child loves the fire.

The Picture of Dorian Gray
CHAPTER SEVENTEEN

Children begin by loving their parents; after a time they judge them. Rarely, if ever, do they forgive them.

A Woman of No Importance
ACTS TWO AND FOUR

Hesitation of any kind is a sign of mental decay in the young, of physical weakness in the old.

The Importance of Being Earnest
ACT FOUR

To lose one parent may be regarded as a misfortune … to lose both looks like carelessness.

The Importance of Being Earnest
ACT ONE

As soon as people are old enough to know better, they don't know anything at all.

Lady Windermere's Fan
ACT TWO

Dullness is the coming of age of seriousness.

*Phrases and Philosophies
for the Use of the Young*

Nothing ages like happiness.

An Ideal Husband
ACT ONE

Health is the primary duty of life.

The Importance of Being Earnest
ACT ONE

What a pity that in life we only get our lessons when they are of no use to us.

Lady Windermere's Fan
ACT FOUR

At every single moment of one's life one is what one is going to be no less than what one has been.

De Profundis

No life is spoiled but one whose growth is arrested.

The Picture of Dorian Gray
CHAPTER SIX

The soul is born old but grows young. That is the comedy of life. And the body is born young and grows old. That is life's tragedy.

A Woman of No Importance
ACT ONE

Other People

If you pretend to be good, the world takes you very seriously. If you pretend to be bad, it doesn't. Such is the astounding stupidity of optimism.

Lady Windermere's Fan
ACT ONE

Nothing is so aggravating as calmness. There is something positively brutal about the good temper of most modern men.

A Woman of No Importance
ACT TWO

Good people do a great deal of harm in this world. Certainly the greatest harm they do is that they make badness of such extraordinary importance.

Lady Windermere's Fan
ACT ONE

It is always painful to part from people whom one has known for a very brief space of time. The absence of old friends one can endure with equanimity. But even a momentary separation from anyone to whom one has just been introduced is almost unbearable.

The Importance of Being Earnest
ACT THREE

It is perfectly monstrous the way people go about nowadays, saying things against one behind one's back that are absolutely true.

The Picture of Dorian Gray
CHAPTER FIFTEEN

Perhaps, after all, America never has been discovered... I myself would say that it had merely been detected.

The Picture of Dorian Gray
CHAPTER THREE

The youth of America is their oldest tradition. It has been going on now for three hundred years. To hear them talk one would imagine that they were in their first childhood. As far as civilisation goes they are in their second.

A Woman of No Importance
ACT ONE

'They say that when good Americans die they go to Paris.'
'Really! And where do bad Americans go to when they die?'
'They go to America.'

The Picture of Dorian Gray
CHAPTER THREE

It is absurd to divide people into good and bad. People are either charming or tedious.

Lady Windermere's Fan
ACT ONE

The world is simply divided into two classes – those who believe the incredible, like the public – and those who do the improbable.

A Woman of No Importance
ACT THREE

I am not sure that foreigners...should cultivate likes or dislikes about the people they are invited to meet.

A Woman of No Importance
ACT ONE

One can always be kind to people about whom one cares nothing.

The Picture of Dorian Gray
CHAPTER EIGHT

Most people are other people. Their thoughts are someone else's opinions, their life a mimicry, their passions a quotation.

De Profundis

Philanthropic people lose all sense of humanity. It is their distinguishing characteristic.

The Picture of Dorian Gray
CHAPTER THREE

I can't help detesting my relations. I suppose it comes from the fact that none of us can stand other people having the same faults as ourselves.

The Picture of Dorian Gray
CHAPTER ONE

I love hearing my relations abused. It is the only thing that makes me put up with them at all. Relations are simply a tedious pack of people, who haven't got the remotest knowledge of how to live, nor the smallest instinct about when to die.

The Importance of Being Earnest
ACT ONE

I love scandals about other people, but scandals about myself don't interest me. They have not got the charm of novelty.

The Picture of Dorian Gray
CHAPTER TWELVE

It is only shallow people who require years to get rid of an emotion. A man who is master of himself can end a sorrow as easily as he can invent a pleasure.

The Picture of Dorian Gray
CHAPTER NINE

Oh, I like tedious, practical subjects. What I don't like are tedious, practical people. There is a wide difference.

An Ideal Husband
ACT ONE

There is always something infinitely mean about other people's tragedies.

The Picture of Dorian Gray
CHAPTER FOUR

Whenever people agree with me, I always feel I must be wrong.

Lady Windermere's Fan
ACT THREE

The more one analyses people, the more all reasons for analysis disappear.

The Decay of Lying

It is only the intellectually lost who ever argue.

The Picture of Dorian Gray
CHAPTER ONE

My own business always bores me to death. I prefer other people's.

Lady Windermere's Fan
ACT THREE

I like talking to a brick wall – it's the only thing in the world that never contradicts me!

Lady Windermere's Fan
ACT THREE

I choose my friends for their good looks, my acquaintances for their good characters, and my enemies for their good intellects. A man cannot be too careful in the choice of his enemies.

The Picture of Dorian Gray
CHAPTER ONE

Fashion is what one wears oneself. What is unfashionable is what other people wear.

An Ideal Husband
ACT THREE

Whatever happens to another happens to oneself.

De Profundis

What people call insincerity is simply a method by which we can multiply our personalities.

The Critic as Artist

Laughter is not at all a bad beginning for a friendship, and is far the best ending for one.

> *The Picture of Dorian Gray*
> CHAPTER ONE

There is no reason why a man should show his life to the world. The world does not understand things.

> *De Profundis*

I never approve, or disapprove, of anything new. It is an absurd attitude to take towards life. We are not sent into the world to air our moral prejudices. I never take any notice of what common people say, and I never interfere with what charming people do.

> *The Picture of Dorian Gray*
> CHAPTER SIX

I don't like principles ... I prefer prejudices.

> *An Ideal Husband*
> ACT FOUR

What is said of a man is nothing. The point is, who says it.

> *De Profundis*

If there was less sympathy in the world there would be less trouble in the world.

> *An Ideal Husband*
> ACT THREE

The well-bred contradict other people. The wise contradict themselves.

> *Phrases and Philosophies*
> *for the Use of the Young*

There is the same world for all of us, and good and evil, sin and innocence, go through it hand in hand. To shut one's eyes to half of life that one may live securely is as though one blinded oneself that one might walk with more safety in a land of pit and precipice.

> *Lady Windermere's Fan*
> ACT FOUR

Morals & Religion

One regrets the loss of even one's worst habits.
Perhaps one regrets them the most. They are such an
essential part of one's personality.

The Picture of Dorian Gray
CHAPTER NINETEEN

I can resist everything except temptation.

Lady Windermere's Fan
ACT ONE

Well, I know, of course, how important it is not to
keep a business engagement, if one wants to retain
any sense of the beauty of life.

The Importance of Being Earnest
ACT TWO

When we are happy we are always good, but when
we are good we are not always happy.

The Picture of Dorian Gray
CHAPTER SIX

Indiscretion is the better part of valour.

The Critic as Artist

It is a very dangerous thing to listen. If one listens one
may be convinced; and a man who allows himself to
be convinced by an argument is a thoroughly
unreasonable person.

An Ideal Husband
ACT ONE

Manners before morals!

Lady Windermere's Fan
ACT FOUR

Man is least himself when he talks in his own person. Give him a mask, and he will tell you the truth.

The Critic as Artist

Morality is simply the attitude we adopt towards people whom we personally dislike.

An Ideal Husband
ACT TWO

Anything becomes a pleasure if one does it too often.

The Picture of Dorian Gray
CHAPTER NINETEEN

The only difference between a saint and a sinner is that every saint has a past, and every sinner has a future.

A Woman of No Importance
ACT THREE

The basis for every scandal is an immoral certainty.

The Picture of Dorian Gray
CHAPTER EIGHTEEN

Sentiment is all very well for the buttonhole. But the essential thing for a necktie is style. A well-tied tie is the first serious step in life.

A Woman of No Importance
ACT THREE

One should never take sides in anything ... Taking sides is the beginning of sincerity, and earnestness follows shortly afterwards, and the human being becomes a bore.

A Woman of No Importance
ACT ONE

In the soul of one who is ignorant there is always room for a great idea.

De Profundis

Actions are the first tragedy in life, words are the second.

Lady Windermere's Fan
ACT FOUR

Beauty, real beauty, ends where intellectual expression begins.

The Picture of Dorian Gray
CHAPTER ONE

Beauty is a form of Genius – is higher, indeed, than Genius, as it needs no explanation.

The Picture of Dorian Gray
CHAPTER TWO

I can believe in anything, provided that it is quite incredible.

The Picture of Dorian Gray
CHAPTER ONE

In the English Church a man succeeds, not through his capacity for belief, but through his capacity for disbelief. Ours is the only Church where the sceptic stands at the altar, and where St Thomas is regarded as the ideal apostle.

The Decay of Lying

Conscience and cowardice are really the same things... Conscience is the trade name of the firm. That is all.

The Picture of Dorian Gray
CHAPTER ONE

All crime is vulgar, just as all vulgarity is crime.

The Picture of Dorian Gray
CHAPTER NINETEEN

What is a cynic? a man who knows the price of everything and the value of nothing.

Lady Windermere's Fan
ACT THREE

For a dreamer is one who can only find his way by moonlight, and his punishment is that he sees the dawn before the rest of the world.

The Critic as Artist

Duty ... most barren of all bonds between man and man.

De Profundis

In the strangely simple economy of the world people only get what they give, and to those who have not enough imagination to penetrate the mere outward of things and feel pity, what pity can be given save that of scorn?

De Profundis

Experience is the name every one gives to their mistakes.

Lady Windermere's Fan
ACT THREE

I am not myself in favour of premature experience.

The Importance of Being Earnest
ACT FOUR

If one doesn't talk about a thing, it has never happened. It is simply expression ... that gives reality to things.

The Picture of Dorian Gray
CHAPTER NINE

Remember that one should be thankful that there is any fault of which one can be unjustly accused.

De Profundis

Misfortunes one can endure – they come from outside, they are accidents. But to suffer for one's own faults – ah! – there is the sting of life.

Lady Windermere's Fan
ACT ONE

I can stand brute force, but brute reason is quite unbearable. There is something unfair about its use. It is hitting below the intellect.

The Picture of Dorian Gray
CHAPTER THREE

We are never less free than when we try to act.
The Critic as Artist

To be entirely free, and at the same time entirely dominated by law, is the eternal paradox of human life.

De Profundis

Remember that the fool in the eyes of the gods and the fool in the eyes of man are very different.
De Profundis

The real fool, such as the gods mock or mar, is he who does not know himself.
De Profundis

Those who have much are often greedy.
De Profundis

We are all in the gutter, but some of us are looking at the stars.

Lady Windermere's Fan
ACT THREE

Nothing should be out of reach of hope. Life is a hope.

A Woman of No Importance
ACT ONE

Ideals are dangerous things. Realities are better.
Lady Windermere's Fan
ACT FOUR

One should always be a little improbable. The improbable is always in bad, or at any rate, questionable taste.

The Importance of Being Earnest
ACT FOUR

Ignorance is like a delicate exotic fruit; touch it and the bloom is gone.

The Importance of Being Earnest
ACT ONE

Industry is the root of all ugliness.

Phrases and Philosophies
for the Use of the Young

All influence is bad, but ... a good influence is the worst in the world.

A Woman of No Importance
ACT FOUR

There is no such thing as a good influence ... All influence is immoral.

The Picture of Dorian Gray
CHAPTER TWO

Intellect is in itself a mode of exaggeration, and destroys the harmony of any face.

The Picture of Dorian Gray
CHAPTER ONE

The intellect is not a serious thing, and never has been. It is an instrument on which one plays, that is all. The only serious form of intellect I know is the British intellect. And on the British intellect the illiterates play the drum.

A Woman of No Importance
ACT ONE

The fatal errors of life are not due to a man's being unreasonable: an unreasonable moment may be one's finest moment. They are due to man's being logical.

De Profundis

Life is simply a *mauvais quart d'heure* made up of exquisite moments.

A Woman of No Importance
ACT TWO

The secret of life is never to have an emotion that is unbecoming.

A Woman of No Importance
ACT THREE

Life is terrible. It rules us, we do not rule it.

Lady Windermere's Fan
ACT FOUR

I am always astonishing myself. It is the only thing that makes life worth living.

A Woman of No Importance
ACT THREE

Once at least in his life each man walks with Christ to Emmaus.

De Profundis

We needs must love the highest when we see it!

An Ideal Husband
ACT ONE

Moderation is a fatal thing. Enough is as bad as a meal. More than enough is as good as a feast.

The Picture of Dorian Gray
CHAPTER FIFTEEN

Everything must come to one out of one's own nature.

De Profundis

It seems to me that we all look at Nature too much, and live with her too little.

De Profundis

The reason we all like to think so well of ourselves is that we are all afraid for ourselves. The basis of optimism is sheer terror.

The Picture of Dorian Gray
CHAPTER SIX

Paradoxes are always dangerous things.

The Decay of Lying

Pleasure is the only thing worth having a theory about.

The Picture of Dorian Gray
CHAPTER SIX

I adore simple pleasures. They are the last refuge of the complex.

A Woman of No Importance
ACT ONE

When the gods wish to punish us they answer our prayers.

An Ideal Husband
ACT TWO

Punctuality is the thief of time.

The Picture of Dorian Gray
CHAPTER FOUR

It is only the superficial qualities that last. Man's deeper nature is soon found out.

The Importance of Being Earnest
ACT THREE

Questions are never indiscreet. Answers sometimes are.

An Ideal Husband
ACT ONE

To test reality we must see it on the tight-rope. When the Verities become acrobats we can judge them.

The Picture of Dorian Gray
CHAPTER THREE

All repetition is anti-spiritual.

De Profundis

Good resolutions are useless attempts to interfere with scientific laws. Their origin is pure vanity. Their result is absolutely *nil* ... They are simply cheques that men draw on a bank where they have no account.

The Picture of Dorian Gray
CHAPTER EIGHT

I love scrapes. They are the only things that are never serious.

The Importance of Being Earnest
ACT ONE

Self-denial is simply a method by which man arrests his progress, and self-sacrifice a survival of the mutilation of the savage.

The Critic as Artist

There is a luxury in self-reproach. When we blame ourselves we feel that no one else has a right to blame us.

The Picture of Dorian Gray
CHAPTER EIGHT

A sentimentalist is simply one who desires to have the luxury of an emotion without paying for it.

De Profundis

Sentimentality is merely the Bank Holiday of cynicism.

De Profundis

The supreme vice is shallowness.

De Profundis

A little sincerity is a dangerous thing, and a great deal of it is absolutely fatal.

The Critic as an Artist
PART TWO

The only horrible thing in the world is *ennui* ... That is the one sin for which there is no forgiveness.

The Picture of Dorian Gray
CHAPTER EIGHTEEN

Sins of the flesh are nothing. They are maladies for physicians to cure, if they should be cured. Sins of the soul alone are shameful.

De Profundis

Nothing can cure the soul but the senses, just as nothing can cure the senses but the soul.

The Picture of Dorian Gray
CHAPTER TWO

To become the spectator of one's own life ... is to escape the suffering of life.

The Picture of Dorian Gray
CHAPTER NINE

There is no sin except stupidity.

The Critic as Artist

It is far more difficult to talk about a thing than to do it.

The Critic as Artist

The only way to get rid of a temptation is to yield to it.

The Picture of Dorian Gray
CHAPTER TWO

There is no secret of life. Life's aim, if it has one, is simply to be always looking for temptation.

A Woman of No Importance
ACT THREE

In a Temple every one should be serious, except the thing that is worshipped.

A Woman of No Importance
ACT ONE

The things one feels absolutely certain about are
never true.

The Picture of Dorian Gray
CHAPTER NINETEEN

All thought is immoral. Its very essence is destruc-
tion. If you think of anything, you kill it. Nothing
survives being thought of.

A Woman of No Importance
ACT THREE

It is better to be beautiful than to be good. But ... it is
better to be good than to be ugly.

The Picture of Dorian Gray
CHAPTER SEVENTEEN

The world has been made by fools that wise men
should live in it!

A Woman of No Importance
ACT THREE

Books

The books that the world calls immoral are books that show the world its own shame.

The Picture of Dorian Gray
CHAPTER NINETEEN

Meredith is a prose Browning, and so is Browning. He used poetry as a medium for writing in prose.

The Critic as Artist

The good ended happily, and the bad unhappily. That is what Fiction means.

The Importance of Being Earnest
ACT TWO

It must be perfectly easy in half an hour to say whether a book is worth anything or worth nothing. Ten minutes are really sufficient, if one has the instinct for form.

The Critic as Artist

Are there ever any ideas in improving books? I fear not.

The Importance of Being Earnest
ACT THREE

The transformation of Dr Jekyll reads dangerously like an experiment out of the *Lancet*.

The Decay of Lying

As for modern journalism, it is not my business to defend it. It justifies its own existence by the great Darwinian principle of the survival of the vulgarest. I have merely to do with literature.

The Critic as Artist

'What is the difference between literature and journalism?'
'Oh! journalism is unreadable, and literature is not read. That is all.'

The Critic as Artist

From the point of view of literature Mr Kipling is a genius who drops his aspirates.

The Critic as Artist

Ah! Meredith! Who can define him? His style is chaos illuminated by flashes of lightning. As a writer he has mastered everything except language: as a novelist he can do everything except tell a story: as an artist he is everything except articulate.

The Decay of Lying

There is no such thing as a moral or an immoral book. Books are well written, or badly written. That is all.

The Picture of Dorian Gray
PREFACE

Anybody can write a three-volume novel. It merely requires a complete ignorance of both life and literature.

The Critic as Artist

I quite admit that modern novels have many good points. All I insist on is that, as a class, they are quite unreadable.

The Decay of Lying

One should read everything. More than half of modern culture depends on what one shouldn't read.

The Importance of Being Earnest
ACT ONE

One should always have something sensational to read in the train.

The Importance of Being Earnest
ACT THREE

What are American dry goods? American novels.

A Woman of No Importance
ACT ONE

The only artists I have ever known, who are personally delightful, are bad artists. Good artists exist simply in what they make, and consequently are perfectly uninteresting in what they are.

The Picture of Dorian Gray
CHAPTER FOUR

Education is an admirable thing, but it is as well to remember from time to time, that nothing that is worth knowing can be taught.

A Few Maxims for the Instruction
of the Over-Educated

Nothing refines but the intellect.

A Woman of No Importance
ACT THREE

As a rule, I dislike modern memoirs. They are generally written by people who have either entirely lost their memories, or have never done anything worth remembering.

The Critic as Artist

I never quarrel with actions. My one quarrel is with words. That is the reason I hate vulgar realism in literature. The man who would call a spade a spade should be compelled to use one. It is the only thing he is fit for.

The Picture of Dorian Gray
CHAPTER SEVENTEEN

The truth is rarely pure and never simple. Modern life would be very tedious if it were either, and modern literature a complete impossibility!

The Importance of Being Earnest
ACT ONE

Art & Music

It is not good for one's morals to see bad acting.

The Picture of Dorian Gray
CHAPTER SEVEN

It is only an auctioneer who can equally and impartially admire all schools of Art.

The Critic as Artist

In art good intentions are not of the smallest value. All bad art is the result of good intentions.

De Profundis

No great artist ever sees things as they really are. If he did he would cease to be an artist.

The Decay of Lying

Art never expresses anything but itself.

The Decay of Lying

A subject that is beautiful in itself gives no suggestion to the artist. It lacks imperfection.

*A Few Maxims for the Instruction
of the Over-Educated*

After playing Chopin, I feel as if I had been weeping over sins that I had never committed, and mourning over tragedies that were not my own.

The Critic as Artist

I don't play accurately – any one can play accurately – but I play with wonderful expression. As far as the piano is concerned, sentiment is my forte. I keep science for Life.

The Importance of Being Earnest
ACT ONE

As art springs from personality, so it is only to personality that it can be revealed, and from the meeting of the two comes right interpretative criticism.

The Critic as Artist

Mediocrity weighing mediocrity in the balance, and incompetence applauding its brother – that is the spectacle which the artistic activity of England affords us from time to time.

The Critic as Artist

The moral life of man forms part of the subject-matter of the artist, but the morality of art consists in the perfect use of an imperfect medium.

The Picture of Dorian Gray
PREFACE

Whatever music sounds like, I am glad to say that it does not sound in the smallest degree like German.

The Critic as Artist

Music makes one feel so romantic – at least it always gets on one's nerves.

A Woman of No Importance
ACT FOUR

I never talk during music, at least during good music. If one hears bad music, it is one's duty to drown it in conversation.

The Picture of Dorian Gray
CHAPTER FOUR

If one plays good music, people don't listen, and if one plays bad music people don't talk.

The Importance of Being Earnest
ACT ONE

Music is the perfect type of art. Music can never reveal its ultimate secret.

The Critic as Artist

Musical people are so absurdly unreasonable. They always want one to be perfectly dumb when one is longing to be absolutely deaf.

An Ideal Husband
ACT TWO

The Philistine element in life is not the failure to understand Art. Charming people such as fishermen, shepherds, ploughboys, peasants and the like know nothing about Art, and are the very salt of the earth.

De Profundis

Every single work of art is the fulfilment of a prophecy.

De Profundis

There is no fine art without self-consciousness, and self-consciousness and the critical spirit are one.

The Critic as Artist

The public is wonderfully tolerant. It forgives everything except genius.

The Critic as Artist

It is a sad thing to think of, but there is no doubt that Genius lasts longer then Beauty. That accounts for the fact that we all take such pains to over-educate ourselves.

The Picture of Dorian Gray
CHAPTER ONE

This unfortunate aphorism about Art holding the mirror up to Nature is deliberately said by Hamlet in order to convince the bystanders of his absolute insanity in all art-matters.

The Decay of Lying

Modern Times

Nowadays people seem to look on life as a speculation. It is not a speculation. It is a sacrament. Its ideal is Love. Its purification is sacrifice.

Lady Windermere's Fan
ACT ONE

Every man of ambition has to fight his century with its own weapons. What this century worships is wealth. The God of this century is wealth.

An Ideal Husband
ACT TWO

All that one should know about modern life is where the Duchesses are; anything else is quite demoralising.

An Ideal Husband
ACT FOUR

To get into the best society, nowadays, one has either to feed people, amuse people, or shock people – that is all!

A Woman of No Importance
ACT THREE

To have been well brought up is a great drawback nowadays. It shuts one out from so much.

A Woman of No Importance
ACT THREE

Nowadays to be intelligible is to be found out.

Lady Windermere's Fan
ACT ONE

To be modern is the only thing worth being nowadays.

A Woman of No Importance
ACT THREE

Nothing is so dangerous as being too modern. One is apt to grow old-fashioned quite suddenly.

An Ideal Husband
ACT TWO

Opium-dens, where one could buy oblivion, dens of horror where the memory of old sins could be destroyed by the madness of sins that were new.

The Picture of Dorian Gray
CHAPTER SIXTEEN

The two weak points in our age are its want of principle and its want of profile.

The Importance of Being Earnest
ACT FOUR

Private information is practically the source of every large modern fortune.

An Ideal Husband
ACT TWO

To pose as a champion of purity, as it is termed, is, in the present condition of the British public, the surest mode of becoming for the nonce a heroic figure.

De Profundis

We live in an age that reads too much to be wise, and that thinks too much to be beautiful.

The Picture of Dorian Gray
CHAPTER EIGHT

We live in an age when unnecessary things are our only necessities.

The Picture of Dorian Gray
CHAPTER SEVEN

Only people who look dull ever get into the House of Commons, and only people who are dull ever succeed there.

An Ideal Husband
ACT FOUR

There is hardly a single person in the House of Commons worth painting; though many of them would be better for a little white-washing.

The Picture of Dorian Gray
CHAPTER SIX

The House of Commons really does very little harm. You can't make people good by Act of Parliament – that is something.

A Woman of No Importance
ACT ONE

Really, now that the House of Commons is trying to become useful, it does a great deal of harm.

An Ideal Husband
ACT ONE

Democracy simply means the bludgeoning of the people by the people for the people.

The Soul of Man under Socialism

We in the House of Lords are never in touch with public opinion. That makes us a civilised body.

A Woman of No Importance
ACT ONE

Really, if the lower orders don't set us a good example, what on earth is the use of them?

The Importance of Being Earnest
ACT ONE

I adore political parties. They are the only place left to us where people don't talk politics.

An Ideal Husband
ACT ONE

I delight in talking politics. I talk them all day long.
But I can't bear listening to them. I don't know how
the unfortunate men in the House stand these long
debates.

An Ideal Husband
ACT ONE

The real tragedy of the poor is that they can afford
nothing but self-denial. Beautiful sins, like beautiful
things, are the privilege of the rich.

The Picture of Dorian Gray
CHAPTER SIX

As for the virtuous poor, one can pity them, of
course, but one cannot possibly admire them.

The Soul of Man under Socialism

As long as war is regarded as wicked, it will always
have its fascination. When it is looked upon as
vulgar, it will cease to be popular.

The Critic as Artist

The growing influence of women is the one
reassuring thing in our political life.

A Woman of No Importance
ACT ONE

When a man says that he has exhausted Life, one
knows that life has exhausted him.

The Picture of Dorian Gray
CHAPTER FIFTEEN

One must be serious about something if one wants to
have any amusement in life.

The Importance of Being Earnest
ACT THREE

Three addresses always inspire perfect confidence,
even in tradesmen.

The Importance of Being Earnest
ACT FOUR

When one is in town one amuses oneself. When one is in the country one amuses other people. It is excessively boring.

The Importance of Being Earnest
ACT ONE

It is very vulgar to talk about one's business. Only people like stock-brokers do that, and then merely at dinner parties.

The Importance of Being Earnest
ACT THREE

Nowadays we are all of us so hard up, that the only pleasant things to pay *are* compliments. They're the only things we *can* pay.

Lady Windermere's Fan
ACT ONE

Learned conversation is either the affectation of the ignorant or the profession of the mentally unemployed.

The Critic as Artist

Anybody can be good in the country.

The Picture of Dorian Gray
CHAPTER NINETEEN

It is very vulgar to talk like a dentist when one isn't a dentist. It produces a false impression.

The Importance of Being Earnest
ACT ONE

To be popular one must be a mediocrity.

The Picture of Dorian Gray
CHAPTER SEVENTEEN

One can survive anything nowadays, except death, and live down anything except a good reputation.

A Woman of No Importance
ACT ONE

Never speak disrespectfully of Society ... Only people who can't get into it do that.

> *The Importance of Being Earnest*
> ACT FOUR

Talk to every woman as if you loved her, and to every man as if he bored you, and at the end of your first season, you will have the reputation of possessing the most perfect social tact.

> *A Woman of No Importance*
> ACT THREE

In my young days ... one never met any one in society who worked for their living. It was not considered the thing.

> *A Woman of No Importance*
> ACT ONE

The English country gentleman galloping after a fox – the unspeakable in full pursuit of the uneatable.

> *A Woman of No Importance*
> ACT ONE

A man whose desire is to be something separate from himself, to be a Member of Parliament, or a successful grocer, or a prominent solicitor, or a judge, or something equally tedious, invariably succeeds in being what he wants to be. That is his punishment. Those who want a mask have to wear it.

> *De Profundis*

If one puts forward an idea to a true Englishman – always a rash thing to do – he never dreams of considering whether the idea is right or wrong. The only thing he considers of any importance is whether one believes it oneself.

> *A Picture of Dorian Gray*
> CHAPTER ONE

Nowadays most people die of a sort of creeping common sense, and discover when it is too late that the only things one never regrets are one's mistakes.

The Picture of Dorian Gray
CHAPTER ONE

London is too full of fogs and ... serious people ... Whether the fogs produce the serious people or whether the serious people produce the fogs, I don't know.

Lady Windermere's Fan
ACT FOUR

Society, civilised society at least, is never very ready to believe anything to the detriment of those who are both rich and fascinating.

The Picture of Dorian Gray
CHAPTER ELEVEN

A cigarette is the perfect type of a perfect pleasure. It is exquisite, and it leaves one unsatisfied. What more can one want?

The Picture of Dorian Gray
CHAPTER SIX

I feel sure that if I lived in the country for six months, I should become so unsophisticated that no one would take the slightest notice of me.

A Woman of No Importance
ACT ONE

A man who can dominate a London dinner-table can dominate the world. The future belongs to the dandy. It is the exquisites who are going to rule.

A Woman of No Importance
ACT THREE

The first duty in life is to be as artificial as possible. What the second is, no one has yet discovered.

*Phrases and Philosophies
for the Use of the Young*

England will never be civilised till she has added Utopia to her dominions.

The Critic as Artist

Nothing succeeds like excess.

A Woman of No Importance
ACT THREE

To invent anything at all is an act of sheer genius, and, in a commercial age like ours, shows considerable physical courage.

The Importance of Being Earnest
ACT FOUR

Land has ceased to be either a profit or a pleasure. It gives one position, and prevents one from keeping it up.

The Importance of Being Earnest
ACT ONE

Lying for the sake of a monthly salary is, of course, well known in Fleet Street.

The Decay of Lying

Do you believe all that is written in the newspaper? I do. Nowadays it is only the unreadable that occurs.

A Woman of No Importance
ACT ONE

You should study the Peerage ... It is the one book a young man about town should know thoroughly, and it is the best thing in fiction the English have ever done.

A Woman of No Importance
ACT THREE

What is the difference between scandal and gossip? Oh! gossip is charming! History is merely gossip. But scandal is gossip made tedious by morality. A man who moralises is usually a hypocrite, and a woman who moralises is invariably plain.

Lady Windermere's Fan
ACT THREE

Society takes upon itself the right to inflict appalling punishments on the individual, but it also has the supreme vice of shallowness, and fails to realise what it has done.

De Profundis

Oh! spies are of no use nowadays. Their profession is over. The newspapers do their work instead.

An Ideal Husband
ACT THREE

There is only one thing in the world worse than being talked about, and that is not being talked about.

The Picture of Dorian Gray
CHAPTER ONE

Thinking is the most unhealthy thing in the world, and people die of it just as they die of any other disease. Fortunately, in England at any rate, thought is not catching. Our splendid physique as a people is entirely due to our national stupidity.

The Decay of Lying

In this world there are only two tragedies. One is not getting what one wants, and the other is getting it.

Lady Windermere's Fan
ACT THREE

One must have some occupation nowadays. If I hadn't my debts I shouldn't have anything to think about.

A Woman of No Importance
ACT ONE